Jacine Star

OVERCOMING SUICIDAL THOUGHTS

A Christian Guide to Overcoming Suicidal Thoughts and Finding Purpose

Contents

Introduction

Finding Hope and Meaning Amid Adversity

Life is a priceless treasure woven with exquisite strands of joy, love, and purpose. However, there are moments when the weight of sadness becomes too much to bear, spreading a smothering shadow over our hearts and minds. Suicidal thoughts can grab us in these moments, robbing us of hope and clouding our picture of the future.

But, dear reader, there is a light that shines through even the thickest fog amid your agony and gloom. It is the light of faith, the guiding hand of a loving Creator who longs to restore your hope and guide you to a life of meaning.

This book, ***"Overcoming Suicidal Thoughts: A Christian Guide to Overcoming Suicidal Thoughts***," was written by a Christian to overcome Suicidal Thoughts and Find Purpose," it is written with profound compassion and firm confidence in God's Word's transformative power. It is an invitation to travel alongside other passengers who have experienced the desolation of suicidal thoughts and found the strength to overcome them.

Within these pages, you will find comfort and direction based on Jesus Christ's teachings and the knowledge of Scripture. This book is intended to provide you with practical methods and spiritual insights to help you navigate the depths of despair, accept recovery, and discover the unique purpose that God has ordained for your life.

We will go over your difficulties chapter by chapter, presenting a Christian perspective on understanding and conquering suicidal thoughts. We will embark on an adventure, rediscovering God's purpose for your existence, reminding you of your great worth in His eyes, and lighting a flame of hope within your heart.

Furthermore, we will discuss the importance of supporting your mental and spiritual well-being, since true recovery requires an integrated approach. We will investigate the power of prayer, the significance of getting professional assistance, and the transforming potential of a supportive Christian community.

It is critical to recognize that the road to conquering suicidal thoughts may be long and difficult. However, with each page turn, you will discover a reservoir of strength that defies human comprehension. You are never alone in your trials as a Christian. The God who made you is right there with you, waiting to lift you up and give you hope.

May this book serve as a beacon of light, leading you toward the bountiful life that lies beyond the darkness. May it remind you of your intrinsic worth, your unique mission, and God's limitless love for you.

Allow faith to overcome despair and hope to triumph as we embark on this momentous journey together. Even in the darkest of nights, a fresh day is only beyond the horizons

Chapter 1

Understanding suicidal thoughts through a Christian Lens

What is suicide and how it affects a believer?

Suicide is a tragic and extremely complex act in which a person purposefully kills themselves. As a believer, the concept of suicide and its consequences has special meaning and influence. It is critical to approach this subject with compassion, empathy, and sensitivity, acknowledging the enormous sorrow and challenges that drive someone to ponder or commit such a heinous act.

Death and the Divine Image

According to the Christian faith, life is a valuable gift from God, and each human being is formed in the divine image. Suicide represents the taking of one's own life, which God has individually designed and deemed important. It breaks my heart and the heart of God, who wishes for all His children to have abundant life (John 10:10).

In opposition to God's Plan and Purpose

Suicide is counter to God's plan and purpose for His children. The act of purposefully taking one's own life shatters the potential for growth, healing, and the fulfillment of God's intentions for that person. It keeps the person from experiencing the richness of life and the opportunities for transformation and service that God has in store for them.

Emotional Impact on Family Members

Family members, friends, and loved ones are left to deal with great grief, uncertainty, guilt, and a slew of other complex emotions. The suddenness of loss exacerbates the pain of loss, which frequently leaves loved ones with unanswered questions and a strong sense of loss.

The Effect on the Christian Community

Suicide can also have serious consequences for the Christian community. It can test and disturb fellow believers' faith, causing them to doubt God's goodness, His plan, and the efficiency of their prayers. The Christian community must unite in offering support, love, and understanding to people affected by suicide or the thoughts of suicide, as well as seeking healing and reconciliation as a group of believers.

Recognizing Mental Health

It is critical to approach the subject of suicide with knowledge of mental health issues. Suicidal thoughts are frequently triggered by intense emotional suffering, mental health issues, or significant internal conflicts that people may confront. Mental health concerns are complex and necessitate professional assessment, treatment, and care. As Christians, we must give empathy, compassion, and resources to those who are dealing with mental health issues.

Seeking Healing and Redemption from God

While suicide causes enormous anguish and has terrible consequences, it is critical to remember that God's grace and redeeming power reach even to the depths of human suffering. God is a healer, a comforter, and a fixer of shattered things. He is there in the midst of our suffering and offers those who seek Him hope, healing, and restoration.

We must extend God's love, mercy, and compassion to those in need. We are called to establish safe areas for people to discuss their concerns, seek treatment, and find support. We may offer peace, hope, and a reminder of God's unwavering presence via prayer, love, and the power of community.

As a believer, suicide has serious consequences. It is a devastating loss of life that runs counter to God's plan and purpose. It has an impact on people's loved ones as well as the Christian community. Despite the anguish and destruction, we can hold on to God's love and seek His healing and redemption. Let us provide understanding, compassion, and assistance to those in need, representing Christ's love in a world that sorely needs His light.

Suicidal Thoughts Through a Christian Lens

Understanding suicidal thoughts through a Christian lens can provide a unique perspective that offers hope, consolation, and a route to healing in times of deep sorrow and overwhelming darkness. As we embark on this journey, we will explore the depths of sorrow and misery that those experiencing suicidal thoughts frequently face, finding solace and insight in Jesus Christ's teachings and the wisdom contained in Scripture.

1.1 The Purity of Life

The belief in the sanctity of life is central to the Christian worldview. Humanity is created in the image of God, according to Genesis 1:27: "So God created mankind in his own image, in the image of God he created them; male and female he created them." This the divine imprint on every human being confers inherent worth and value, regardless of their circumstances or hardships. Recognizing this truth is critical to comprehending suicidal thoughts.

When we are struggling with suicidal thoughts, it is critical to realize that our lives have significance and purpose. God's close involvement in our creation is vividly expressed in Psalm 139:13-14: "For you created my inmost being; you knit me together in my mother's womb." I praise you because I am fearfully and wonderfully formed; I know your works are great." Our existence is not haphazard or random; rather, it is meticulously planned by a loving Creator who has a specific plan for each of us.

1.2 The Mental Battle

A strong sense of hopelessness, sorrow, and misguided thinking is often at the root of these behaviors. In his letter to the Romans, the apostle Paul admits the internal conflict that can devour us: "I do not understand what I do." "I do not do what I want to do, but I do what I despise" (Romans 7:15). This paragraph reminds us that our brains may be a battleground for unpleasant thoughts and emotions.

As Christians, we are obligated to guard our hearts and minds, as Paul advises in Philippians 4:8: "Finally, brothers and sisters, whatever is true, noble, right, pure, lovely, admirable—if anything is excellent or praiseworthy—think about such things." By reorganizing our thoughts, we may combat the darkness that wants to overwhelm our brains by focusing on what is good, noble, and aligned with God's truth.

1.3 God's Promises and the Gift of Hope

In the face of tremendous despair brought on by suicidal thoughts, the Christian faith offers the gift of hope—hope that transcends our current circumstances and guides us to a future full of promise. "For I know the plans I have for you," says the

Lord, "plans to prosper you and not harm you, plans to give you hope and a future."

Furthermore, Jesus reminds us of His constant presence and the comfort He provides in times of adversity. "And surely," He promises in Matthew 28:20. I will be with you till the end of time." This certainty reminds us that we are not alone, even in our darkest situations. The God of all comfort (2 Corinthians 1:3) understands our anguish and extends His loving embrace to all who seek Him.

1.4 Dealing with Faith and Purpose Issues

Suicidal thoughts might raise deep existential questions about the meaning and purpose of existence. King Solomon wrestles with the futility of earthly pursuits and the emptiness they can bring in Ecclesiastes. In Ecclesiastes 12:13, he finishes with wisdom: "Now all has been heard; here is the conclusion of the matter: Fear God and keep his commandments, for this is the duty of all mankind." Embracing a relationship with God and obeying His commands can give our lives meaning and purpose.

Furthermore, we are called to love and serve others as Christians. In Matthew 22:37-39, Jesus Himself declared the greatest commandments: "'Love the Lord your God with all your heart, soul, and mind." This is the first and most important commandment. "The second is similar: 'Love your neighbor as yourself.'" We engage in God's redeeming mission by seeking opportunities to love and support those around us, discovering significance and fulfillment even in the midst of our own hardships.

In our quest to understand suicidal thoughts through a Christian perspective, it is critical to realize that mental health is complex, and obtaining professional treatment is a good place to start. This is a critical phase in the healing process. While integrating religion ideas into the healing process, Christian counselors, therapists, and pastors can provide important support and assistance.

As we continue our investigation, keep in mind that analyzing suicidal thoughts from a Christian viewpoint provides a context of hope, reminding us of the great value of our lives, the fights we confront within our brains, God's promises, and the transformational power of faith. We will go deeper into these principles in the next chapters, presenting practical insights and scriptural wisdom to aid in overcoming suicidal thoughts and finding enduring purpose in the embrace of our loving Creator

Life's common misconceptions and spiritual challenges

Individuals who are suicidal typically have common beliefs about life and the spiritual challenges they endure. These myths can deepen emotions of hopelessness and obstruct the path to recovery and purpose. Let us dispel some of these myths and shine a light on the truth contained in the Christian religion.

2.1 Misconception: Life Has No Value or Purpose.

One common misperception is that life has no inherent significance or purpose. Personal disappointments, cultural pressures, or a general sense of despair can all contribute to this mindset. It is critical to understand that this notion contradicts biblical teachings.

As Christians, we recognize that God, the Creator of the cosmos, has instilled in us divine attributes, life with value and purpose. We are called to love and serve both God and our fellow humans. This concept is affirmed in Ephesians 2:10, which states, "For we are God's handiwork, created in Christ

Jesus to do good works, which God prepared in advance for us to do." Regardless of our circumstances or perceived failings, every one of us has a unique role to play in God's ultimate plan, and our lives have immense significance.

2.2 Misconception: Faith Provides Insulation from Life's Trials and Tribulations.

Another common myth is that faith in Christ protects believers from grief, suffering, and spiritual conflicts. While faith provides consolation, hope, and resilience, Scripture warns that in this fallen world, we will endure trials and afflictions.

Jesus himself said "In this world, you will have trouble," He said in John 16:33. But don't despair! "I have triumphed over the world." Our religion as Christians does not exempt us from obstacles; rather, it prepares us to face them with the knowledge that we are not alone. Through life's storms, our faith offers us strength, tranquility, and wisdom. As James 1:2-4 tells us, it is in such fights that our faith is polished and strengthened: "Consider it pure joy, my brothers and sisters, whenever you face trials of various kinds, because you know that the testing of your faith produces perseverance." Allow persistence to accomplish its work so that you will be mature and complete, wanting nothing."

2.3 Misconception: Spiritual Battles are Solely Internal Struggles

Suicidal people frequently assume that their spiritual fights are completely internal, fought within their own brains and souls. While internal fights are important, it is equally important to recognize that spiritual battles involve external factors.

"For our struggle is not against flesh and blood, but against the rulers, against the authorities, against the powers of this dark world, and against the spiritual forces of evil in the heavenly realms," says Ephesians 6:12. This verse emphasizes that our spiritual fights transcend beyond the physical sphere and involve unseen forces at work. Satan, our adversary, strives to steal, kill, and destroy (John 10:10), employing many strategies to undermine our faith.

Understanding the spiritual nature of these fights reminds us of the need of donning God's armor, as described in Ephesians 6:13-18. This armor, which contains truth, righteousness, faith, salvation, and God's Word, enables us to stand steadfast against the enemy's plans. It also emphasizes the importance of prayer, both for personal spiritual growth and for spiritual defense.

Individuals struggling with suicidal thoughts can obtain a deeper grasp of the intrinsic significance and purpose of their lives, the reality of enduring obstacles as believers, and the spiritual battles they face by recognizing these misconceptions and embracing the truths revealed in Scripture. They can embark on a journey armed with these truths of healing, regeneration, and discovering God's true purpose for their lives.

The Core Cause of Suicidal Thoughts and Viable Solutions

Suicidal thoughts are frequently multidimensional and vary from person to person. It is critical to address this subject sensitively and acknowledge that each person's experiences and problems are unique. While there is no one-size-fits-all answer, there are several elements that can lead to suicidal thoughts, as well as potential solutions:

Suicidal thoughts are frequently related to mental health conditions such as depression, anxiety, bipolar disorder, or **post-traumatic stress disorder (PTSD)**. Prioritizing mental health and seeking professional help from therapists, counselors, or psychiatrists who can provide appropriate diagnosis and treatment, which may involve counseling, medication, or a mix of the two, is critical.

Social Isolation and Lack of Support: Loneliness, isolation, and a lack of social support can all play a role in suicide ideation. It is critical to establish a network of helpful relationships. Reaching out to trustworthy friends or family members, joining support groups or communities, seeking counsel from church leaders, or connecting with mental health organizations that provide resources and support can all be part of this process.

Loss, Trauma, and Grief: Significant loss, trauma, or unresolved grief can be extremely unpleasant and contribute to suicide ideation. Seeking professional counseling or therapy to address these emotions, as well as trauma-focused therapy and participation in support groups, can all help with the healing process.

Substance Abuse: Substance abuse or addiction can amplify feelings of despair and helplessness, increasing the likelihood of suicide ideation. Seeking assistance that addresses this core cause requires the utilization of rehabilitation programs, support groups, and counseling specifically geared toward addiction recovery.

Failed Purpose: A spiritual crisis, a crisis of faith, or a lack of meaning and purpose in one's life can cause people to question the worth of their existence. Exploring spiritual activities, participating in meaningful service or volunteering, seeking counsel from spiritual mentors or pastors, and engaging in Bible study can assist individuals in rediscovering their sense of purpose and finding consolation in their relationship with God.

Erroneous Thinking: Suicidal thoughts might come from erroneous thinking patterns such as negative self-perception, pessimism, or feeling trapped. **Cognitive-behavioral therapy (CBT)** can help patients establish healthy coping mechanisms by challenging and reframing these views.

Limiting Access to Lethal Means: such as firearms or drugs can help avoid impulsive acts and provide individuals with critical time to seek treatment during times of crisis.

It is critical to underline that resolving suicidal thoughts necessitates a multifaceted strategy that includes professional assistance, social support, and a personal commitment to self-care and rehabilitation. Promoting community awareness and education, as well as encouraging open dialogues about mental health, are critical measures in avoiding suicide and assisting those in need.

If you or someone you know is having suicidal thoughts, you must seek quick assistance. Contact a helpline, such as the

National Suicide Prevention Lifeline, a mental health professional, or your country's emergency services, as they can assist you provide timely aid and support

Chapter 2

Rediscovering God's Purpose for Your Life

One of the most significant journeys we may start on in the depths of despair is uncovering God's purpose for our existence. When confronted with suicidal thoughts, it is all too easy to lose sight of our intrinsic worth and the unique role we play in God's plan. We can, however, find renewed hope, direction, and a sense of profound significance through the prism of faith. In this chapter, we'll look at the process of finding God's plan for your life and its revolutionary effect.

2.1 Accepting Your Christian Identity

To uncover God's plan for your life, you must first accept your identity in Christ. Knowing who you are as God's child and realizing your mission is dependent on the enormous value, He placed on you. "But you are a chosen people, a royal priesthood, a holy nation, God's special possession," says 1 Peter 2:9, "that you may declare the praises of him who called you out of darkness into his wonderful light." This verse reminds us that we are not average; we have been selected, set apart, and called to declare the glory of God.

By understanding and accepting this identity, you can begin to perceive yourself as valued, adored, and endowed with special gifts and talents to fulfill God's plan for your life. This understanding serves as a solid basis for your journey of rediscovery.

2.2 Seeking God's Direction Through Prayer and Scripture

Seeking God's guidance via prayer and immersing yourself in Scripture is critical as you embark on the journey of rediscovery. You can build a direct connection with God via prayer, revealing your hopes, anxieties, and uncertainties, and seeking His guidance and direction. "Do not be anxious about anything," Philippians 4:6-7 urges us, "but in every situation, by prayer and petition, with thanksgiving, present your requests to God." And the peace of God, which surpasses all comprehension, will keep your hearts and minds in Christ Jesus."

Engaging with Scripture, in addition to prayer, allows you to discover God's truth, promises, and examples of purpose-filled lives. The Bible is a guide that illuminates the route to comprehending God's plan and purpose. "Your word," asserts Psalm 119:105. "Your word is a lamp for my feet and a light on my path." You can obtain insights into God's character, His wishes for His children, and the specific calling He has for you via regular reading, meditation, and study of Scripture.

2.3 Finding Your Gifts, Passions, and Talents

God has uniquely equipped each person with passions, talents, and abilities to carry out His mission. Exploring and embracing these gifts is part of rediscovering God's purpose. According to Romans 12:6-8, "We have different gifts, according to the grace given to each of us... if it is serving, then serve; if it is teaching, then teach." Recognizing your abilities, interests, and hobbies can assist you in determining where you can make a major contribution and bring glory to God.

Consider the activities that bring you joy, energize you, and are consistent with your values. Consider how you can use your talents to help others and advance God's kingdom. God's plan for your life can take many forms, including your work, relationships, ministry, and community involvement. You can enjoy a great sense of fulfillment and joy in your daily pursuits by matching your gifts with God's intentions.

2.4 Accepting a Servant Heart

Adopting a servant's heart is a critical component in rediscovering God's purpose. Throughout His earthly mission, Jesus showed this servant-heartedness. He declared in Mark 10:45, "For even the Son of Man did not come to be served, but to serve, and to give his life." as a ransom for a large number of people." As Christ's followers, we are called to follow in His footsteps by helping others selflessly and compassionately.

Discovering God's purpose frequently entails evaluating how you might positively impact the lives of those around you. It can be done by random acts of kindness, volunteering, mentoring, or using your skills to help others. By living a life of service, you become a conduit for God's love and purpose, influencing lives and altering communities.

2.5 Believing in God's Timing and Providence

Rediscovering God's purpose is not always a quick process. Patience, trust, and faith in God's timing and providence are required. Proverbs 3:5-6 advises us to "trust in the Lord with all your heart and lean not on your understanding. "Submit to him in all your ways, and he will make your pathways straight." Even when the road ahead appears to be uncertain or difficult, trusting in God's guidance and surrendering to His plan permits His purpose to be revealed in due time.

It is critical to realize that God's plan goes beyond our immediate circumstances. He works all things together for good, even the difficulties and setbacks we face along the journey (Romans 8:28). Stay receptive to God's guidance as you walk the process of rediscovery, remembering that His timing is flawless and His intentions for you are rooted in love and wisdom.

Rediscovering God's purpose for your life entails accepting your identity in Christ and seeking His guidance through prayer, reading Scriptures, discovering your abilities and passions, cultivating a servant spirit, and trusting in His time and providence. This rediscovery journey is an ongoing one, characterized by a growing relationship with God and a desire to yield to His will. May you find comfort, hope, and a fresh sense of purpose as you embark on your path, guided by the

One who painstakingly crafted you for a unique and significant role in His perfect plan.

Methods For Keeping Your Mind Pleasant and Distracted from Suicidal Thoughts

Keeping your mind cheerful and distracted from suicidal thoughts is an essential component of dealing with and conquering them. While professional aid and support are necessary, *here are some ways to help you build a positive mentality and refocus your focus:*

Engage in Joy-Inducing Activities: Engage in activities that you enjoy and that produce a sense of satisfaction and fulfillment. Painting, playing an instrument, writing, gardening, or indulging in physical activities such as exercise, dance, or yoga are examples of hobbies. These hobbies can help you divert your attention while also giving you a sense of accomplishment and pleasure.

Develop a Supportive Network: Surround yourself with a supportive network of people, friends, relatives, or support groups who can offer emotional support and understanding are ideal. Having individuals who care about you and can lend a listening ear or words of encouragement can help alleviate loneliness and provide a sense of connection.

Self-Care: Make self-care a priority by engaging in activities that nourish your mind, body, and spirit. This can involve getting adequate sleep, eating a balanced diet, practicing relaxation techniques such as deep breathing or meditation, treating oneself to a warm bath, participating in mindfulness exercises, or spending time in nature. Taking care of yourself holistically can help you feel better mentally.

Seek pleasant Distractions: Participate in activities or hobbies that pique your interest and give pleasant distractions. It could be reading an engrossing book or viewing inspiring movies or television, or indulging in creative activities such as drawing or crafts. These distractions might help you redirect your attention away from negative thoughts and into a happier outlook.

Set Tiny, Achievable Goals: Set tiny, attainable goals for yourself. Breaking larger projects down into manageable pieces can create a sense of purpose, accomplishment, and progress. Celebrate each achievement, no matter how minor, and use it as a springboard to greater things.

Volunteer and Help Others: Performing acts of kindness and assisting others can bring a sense of purpose and contentment.

Volunteering your time and skills for a cause you care about not only benefits others but can also improve your spirits and create a feeling of meaning and connection for you.

Practice Gratitude: Develop a grateful attitude by focusing on the positive parts of your life. Keep a thankfulness diary in which you record the things you are grateful for each day. You can alter your viewpoint to a more optimistic outlook by consciously recognizing and appreciating the gifts and wonderful experiences in your life.

Limit Trigger Exposure: Identify and reduce your exposure to triggers that contribute to negative thoughts or feelings. This could include restricting your exposure to specific news or social media platforms, avoiding stressful places or situations, and being careful of the stuff you consume. Instead, highlight content that is uplifting and motivating and promotes a happy mental state.

Remember that, while these tactics might be beneficial, they are not a replacement for expert assistance. If you are having suicidal thoughts, you must contact a mental health professional, helpline, or support network right away for immediate treatment and counseling.

Chapter 3

Promoting Mental and Spiritual Well-Being

Nurturing both mental and spiritual health is critical on the road to overcoming suicidal thoughts. It is critical to take care of your mind and spirit to discover healing, strength, and resilience. In this chapter, we will look at many tactics and practices that can help you maintain your mental and spiritual well-being while also providing a solid basis for navigating the difficulties you are facing.

3.1 Meditation and Prayer

Prayer and meditation are effective techniques for cultivating spiritual wellness. Prayer helps you to communicate with God, expressing your deepest feelings, anxieties, and hopes. It is a moment to seek guidance, find peace, and connect deeply with the divine. You can entrust your burdens to God through prayer. Meditation, on the other hand, entails quieting the mind, focusing on the present moment, and remaining open to divine revelation.

It can assist to quiet racing thoughts, alleviating worry, and creating inner tranquility. Combining prayer with meditation provides for a more comprehensive approach to spiritual wellness, developing a closer relationship with God, and cultivating a sense of center and clarity.

3.2 Bible Study and Reflection

Scripture study and reflection are vital practices for cultivating spiritual wellness. The Bible is a treasure trove of knowledge, direction, and consolation. It tells us stories of hope, and promises of God's faithfulness, and teaches us in ways that both inspire and challenge us. Engaging with Scripture helps us to align our brains and hearts with God's truth, which promotes spiritual growth and resilience.

Set aside regular time for reading and studying the Bible to nurture your spiritual health. Choose verses that speak to the depth of God's love and purpose for your life or that resonate with your current problems. Consider those scriptures, document your thoughts, and let God's Word influence your perspective, encourage you, and point you in the right way.

3.3 Fellowship and Community

Spiritual wellness is not something that should be pursued alone. Your well-being must participate in community and fellowship with other believers. Seek out a supportive Christian community, such as a local church or small group, where you may connect with others who share your religious journey. These relationships can offer emotional support, accountability, and a sense of belonging.

In the community, you can discuss your problems, receive prayer, and help others. According to Proverbs 27:17, "As iron sharpens iron, so one person sharpens another." You can discover inspiration, advice, and the fortitude to persist in the face of adversity through meaningful connections. Participating in worship services, Bible studies, or Christian events can also help to strengthen your spiritual connection and nourish your soul.

3.4 Emotional Well-Being and Self-Care

Mental health is essential for general well-being and resiliency. Self-care activities that prioritize emotional well-being can have a substantial impact on your ability to overcome suicidal thoughts. Consider the following self-care strategies:

Prioritize restful sleep: Create a calm sleep environment and a consistent sleep habit to support appropriate rest.

Practice stress management: This can be done by incorporating stress-relieving activities, deep breathing exercises, mindfulness meditation, or indulging in calming activities like nature walks or listening to soothing music can be included into your routine.

Seek expert assistance: Contact a mental health expert who can assist you with therapy, counseling, or other evidence-based treatments that are targeted to your specific needs.

Self-awareness: Develop self-awareness of your emotions and good coping techniques, such as journaling, engaging in creative outlets, or talking to a trusted friend or therapist.

Exercise regularly: Regular exercise has been demonstrated to improve mood, anxiety, and overall mental well-being. Find activities that you enjoy, such as walking, dancing, or swimming,

3.5 Develop Gratitude and Positive Thinking

Practicing gratitude and cultivating positive thinking can dramatically improve your mental and physical health as well as your spiritual well-being. Gratitude redirects your emphasis from negativity to recognizing and appreciating your life's benefits. Take time each day to think about what you're grateful for, whether it's small moments of delight, helpful relationships, or acts of kindness.

Furthermore, deliberately establishing positive thinking patterns might help to combat negative ideas and increase resilience. Reframe negative self-talk with positive affirmations and realistic ideas. Philippians 4:8 encourages us to be mindful of "whatever is true, noble, right, pure, lovely, and admirable." You build a fruitful ground for mental and spiritual well-being by deliberately cultivating good thoughts.

Cultivating mental and spiritual health is a transforming practice for overcoming suicidal ideation. You expand your relationship with God through prayer, meditation, scripture study, and reflection, finding solace, guidance, and strength. Participating in supportive Christian groups promotes a sense of belonging as well as emotional support. Making self-care a priority, as well as practicing gratitude and positive thinking, improves your emotional well-being. By taking care of your mental and spiritual health, you open the door to healing, resilience, and a revitalized sense of purpose.

Conclusion

Acceptance of Hope, Purpose, and Healing

We have explored the depths of grief, mental conflicts, and the transformative power of faith in our path of overcoming suicidal thoughts and finding purpose. We've realized that there is hope even in the darkest hours and purpose waiting to be revealed within the depths of our souls via the lens of Christian wisdom and God's Word.

As we come to the end of this book, remember that you are not alone in your troubles. God, the author of life, travels beside you, extending His loving hand to guide you toward healing, purpose, and a bright future. He recognizes your worth, hears your laments, and tenderly holds your heart.

The adventure of overcoming suicidal ideas is not without difficulty. It takes bravery, vulnerability, and dedication to self-care. It is critical to seek professional assistance, participate in supportive networks, and surround yourself with people who can offer love, understanding, and encouragement. Remember that asking for help is not a show of weakness, but rather of your strength and drive to find a better way.

May you continue to invest in practices that offer healing and strength to your mind and soul, and may you continue to cultivate your mental and spiritual health. Allow God's presence to infiltrate your being via prayer, meditation, scripture study, and fellowship, guiding your steps and revealing His purpose for your life.

Remember that purpose is not a fixed goal on your journey of rediscovery, a dynamic, growing experience. It could happen gradually, with fresh chapters and unforeseen twists. Accept the process and submit to God's timing and providence. Trust that God's plan is at work, even in the diversions and setbacks, weaving together the delicate threads of your life to produce a magnificent tapestry.

Hold on to hope as you go forward—the unflinching confidence that a better tomorrow lies. Cling to God's promises of love, fidelity, and redemptive power. Allow hope to be the anchor that keeps you steady amidst the storms, reminding you that you are defined by your strength rather than your troubles.

Finally, may you be a beacon of light and hope as you enter this new chapter of your life. a source of inspiration for others who may be on a similar journey. With compassion and vulnerability, share your stories, your accomplishments, and your newfound purpose. Allow your journey to inspire others, reminding them that they, too, can overcome, find purpose, and experience our Heavenly Father's great love and grace.

May this book be a guide, a friend, and a source of strength for you as you travel to overcome suicidal thoughts and discover the abundant life that God has prepared for you? As you embrace the hope that beyond all comprehension, may you discover healing, meaning, and a deep feeling of contentment.

Remember that you are highly treasured, cherished, and loved. Accept your worth because you are a witness to the human spirit's tenacity and the transformational power of God's grace.

Go forth and live a life of purpose, touching the world with the unique gifts and light that only you can provide, with faith as your guide and hope as your compass. God bless you as you walk this incredible journey of hope, purpose, and healing.